Welcome, fellow word wranglers and phrase flingers, to the wild and wacky world of American slang! If you'[illegible] ever found yourself wondering what on earth your t[illegible]ece meant when she called something "l[illegible]ur coworker keeps saying "spill the t[illegible] no beverage involved, then y[illegible]

This dictionary is your [illegible] evolving linguistic labyrint[illegible] from the quirky to the downright [illegible]iving deep into the phrases that make you [illegible] you know what's up (even if you really, really do[illegible]

Picture this: You're at a party, and someone says, "That guy's got mad skills." Now, you could stand there, nodding awkwardly while internally debating whether to check for a fever, or you could flip open this dictionary and discover that "mad" doesn't mean crazy—it means amazing! Suddenly, you're the life of the party, dropping slang like it's hot and leaving everyone else in the dust.

Whether you're looking to decode your friends' cryptic texts, impress your kids with your hip lingo, or simply have a good laugh at the bizarre ways we humans choose to communicate, this book has got you covered. So buckle up, buttercup, because we're about to take a joyride through the zaniest, funniest, and most colorful expressions this side of the Atlantic.

Remember, language is a living, breathing entity, and slang is its wild child—always changing, always growing, and always ready to make you laugh. So grab your popcorn, get comfy, and let's dive into the crazy world of American slang. Trust us, it's gonna be lit.

INDEX

A

Ace - Meaning excellent or very good.
"He did an ace job on his presentation."
Translation: "He did an excellent job on his presentation."

All-nighter - Staying up all night to study or work.
"I pulled an all-nighter to finish the project."
Translation: "I stayed up all night to finish the project."

Amped - Excited or pumped up.
"I'm so amped for the concert tonight!"
Translation: "I'm so excited for the concert tonight!"

Angsty - Feeling anxious or worried.
"He's been really angsty about the upcoming exams."
Translation: "He's been really anxious about the upcoming exams.

A-game - One's best performance.
"Bring your A-game to the match tomorrow."
Translation: "Give your best performance in the match tomorrow."

Airhead - A foolish or unintelligent person.
"She's such an airhead sometimes."
Translation: "She's so foolish sometimes."

All that - Impressive or excellent.
"She thinks she's all that because she won the contest."
Translation: "She thinks she's impressive because she won the contest."

A-list - The most celebrated or sought-after people.
"He’s on the A-list of Hollywood actors."
Translation: "He’s among the most celebrated Hollywood actors."

All ears - Fully listening.
"I’m all ears, tell me what happened."
Translation: "I'm fully listening, tell me what happened."

Arm candy - An attractive person accompanying someone to an event.
"He showed up to the party with some arm candy."
Translation: "He showed up to the party with an attractive companion."

Awesome - Extremely good or impressive.
"That movie was awesome!"
Translation: "That movie was extremely good!"

Ape - To go crazy or wild.
"He went ape when he found out he won the lottery."
Translation: "He went crazy when he found out he won the lottery."

Awk - Short for awkward.
"That was such an awk moment."
Translation: "That was such an awkward moment."

Ace up one’s sleeve - A hidden advantage.
"He has an ace up his sleeve for the final round."
Translation: "He has a hidden advantage for the final round."

ASAP - As soon as possible.
"I need that report ASAP."
Translation: "I need that report as soon as possible."

Antsy - Impatient or restless.
"The kids are getting antsy waiting for the show to start."
Translation: "The kids are getting restless waiting for the show to start."

Artsy - Showing artistic flair.
"She's really artsy and loves to paint."
Translation: "She's really artistic and loves to paint."

Apple of one's eye - Someone cherished above all others.
"His daughter is the apple of his eye."
Translation: "His daughter is his most cherished person."

Around the bend - Crazy or mad.
"He's been acting like he's around the bend lately."
Translation: "He's been acting crazy lately."

Afterparty - A party that takes place after an event or main party.
"We went to the afterparty after the concert."
Translation: "We went to the party that took place after the concert."

B

Bae - A term of endearment for a significant other.
"I'm going to the movies with my bae tonight."
Translation: "I'm going to the movies with my significant other tonight."

Bail - To leave abruptly.
"I had to bail on the meeting early."
Translation: "I had to leave the meeting early."

Banger - A great song.

"That new track is a banger!"
Translation: "That new track is a great song!"

Beef - Conflict or disagreement.
"They've had beef since high school."
Translation: "They've had a conflict since high school."

Benjamins - Refers to $100 bills.
"He's all about the Benjamins."
Translation: "He's all about the money."

Bet - Agreement or confirmation.
"You want to go to the game? Bet."
Translation: "You want to go to the game? Agreed."

Binge - To do something excessively.
"I binged the entire series last weekend."
Translation: "I watched the entire series excessively last weekend."

Blaze - To smoke marijuana.
"We blazed after the party."
Translation: "We smoked marijuana after the party."

Blow off - To ignore or avoid someone.
"She blew me off at the party."
Translation: "She ignored me at the party."

Boss - Excellent or impressive.
"That car is boss!"
Translation: "That car is excellent!"

Bounce - To leave or depart.
"I'm going to bounce, see you later."
Translation: "I'm going to leave, see you later."

Bougie - Acting high class or fancy.
"She's so bougie with her designer clothes."
Translation: "She's so fancy with her designer clothes."

Bro - A close friend, typically male.
"What's up, bro?"
Translation: "What's up, friend?"

Burn - An insult or witty remark.
"That was a sick burn!"
Translation: "That was a great insult!"

Bust - To fail or be unsuccessful.
"The party was a bust."
Translation: "The party was a failure."

Buzzkill - Something that ruins the mood.
"His negativity is such a buzzkill."
Translation: "His negativity ruins the mood."

BYOB - Bring your own bottle (usually alcohol).
"The party is BYOB."
Translation: "The party requires you to bring your own bottle."

Backseat driver - Someone who offers unsolicited advice.
"I hate backseat drivers."
Translation: "I dislike people who offer unsolicited advice."

Ballin' - Living in luxury or wealth.
"He's been ballin' since he got that promotion."
Translation: "He's been living in luxury since he got that promotion."

Bum - A lazy or incompetent person.
"He's such a bum, he never helps out."
Translation: "He's so lazy, he never helps out."

C

Chill - To relax.
"Let's just chill at my place."
Translation: "Let's just relax at my place."

Clutch - Crucial or essential.
"That save was clutch in the game."
Translation: "That save was crucial in the game."

Cray - Crazy.
"That party was cray!"
Translation: "That party was crazy!"

Cringe - Embarrassing or awkward.
"That joke was so cringe."
Translation: "That joke was so embarrassing."

Crash - To stay overnight at someone's place.
"Can I crash at your place tonight?"
Translation: "Can I stay overnight at your place tonight?"

Creep - A strange or unsettling person.
"That guy is such a creep."
Translation: "That guy is so unsettling."

Croak - To die.
"I thought I was going to croak during that marathon."
Translation: "I thought I was going to die during that marathon."

Cuffed - In a committed relationship.
"He's been cuffed for a year now."

Translation: "He's been in a committed relationship for a year now."

Cutting-edge - Innovative or advanced.
"This new technology is cutting-edge."
Translation: "This new technology is innovative."

Cash - To pay with money.
"Can you cash me out?"
Translation: "Can you pay me?"

Cool beans - Awesome or great.
"You finished the project? Cool beans!"
Translation: "You finished the project? That's great!"

Chop it up - To have a conversation.
"Let's chop it up after the meeting."
Translation: "Let's have a conversation after the meeting."

Cop - To get or obtain something.
"I'm going to cop those new shoes."
Translation: "I'm going to get those new shoes."

Cut - To leave or depart.
"I have to cut early today."
Translation: "I have to leave early today."

Cush - Comfortable or easy.
"This job is pretty cush."
Translation: "This job is pretty comfortable."

Crack up - To laugh uncontrollably.
"That joke made me crack up."

Translation: "That joke made me laugh uncontrollably."

Cray-cray - Extremely crazy.
"That roller coaster was cray-cray!"
Translation: "That roller coaster was extremely crazy!"

Catch some Z's - To sleep.
"I need to catch some Z's before work."
Translation: "I need to sleep before work."

Cheesy - Overly sentimental or corny.
"That movie was so cheesy."
Translation: "That movie was so overly sentimental."

Chillax - To chill and relax.
"Let's just chillax this weekend."
Translation: "Let's just chill and relax this weekend."

D

Dope - Cool or awesome.
"That concert was dope!"
Translation: "That concert was awesome!"

Ditch - To abandon or leave behind.
"Let's ditch this place and go somewhere else."
Translation: "Let's leave this place and go somewhere else."

Dub - To win or succeed.
"We got the dub in the game last night."
Translation: "We won the game last night."

Dead - Extremely funny or hilarious.
"That joke had me dead!"
Translation: "That joke was extremely funny!"

Dank - High quality.
"This pizza is dank."
Translation: "This pizza is high quality."

Dig - To like or appreciate.
"I really dig that song."
Translation: "I really like that song."

Down - To be interested or willing.
"Are you down for a movie tonight?"
Translation: "Are you interested in watching a movie tonight?"

Dude - A guy or friend.

"Hey dude, what's up?"
Translation: "Hey friend, what's up?"

Decked out - Dressed up or decorated.
"She was decked out in a fancy dress."
Translation: "She was dressed up in a fancy dress."

Def - Definitely.
"I'm def going to the party."
Translation: "I'm definitely going to the party."

Dip - To leave.
"Let's dip out of here."
Translation: "Let's leave here."

Diss - To disrespect or insult.
"Don't diss me like that."
Translation: "Don't disrespect me like that."

Down-to-earth - Practical and realistic.
"She's so down-to-earth and easy to talk to."
Translation: "She's so practical and easy to talk to."

Drag - Boring or unpleasant.
"This meeting is such a drag."
Translation: "This meeting is so boring."

Dude - Casual term for a friend or guy.
"Hey dude, what's up?"
Translation: "Hey friend, what's up?"

Deets - Details.
"Can you give me the deets on the party?"

Translation: "Can you give me the details about the party?"
Dough - Money.
"I need to save some dough for the trip."
Translation: "I need to save some money for the trip."

Dime - A very attractive person.
"She's a dime, for sure."
Translation: "She's very attractive, for sure."

Donezo - Finished or done.
"This project is donezo."
Translation: "This project is finished."

Deadbeat - A lazy or irresponsible person.
"He's such a deadbeat, never does anything productive."
Translation: "He's so lazy, never does anything productive."

E

Epic - Grand or impressive.
"That was an epic performance!"
Translation: "That was a grand performance!"

Eats - Food.
"Let's go grab some eats."
Translation: "Let's go grab some food."

Ego trip - An act of boosting one's own ego.
"His speech was just an ego trip."
Translation: "His speech was just to boost his own ego."

Eh - Indifference or mild agreement.
"It's an okay movie, eh."
Translation: "It's an okay movie, I guess."

Extra - Over the top or excessive.
"She's so extra with her reactions."
Translation: "She's so over the top with her reactions."

Epic fail - A spectacular failure.
"That attempt was an epic fail."
Translation: "That attempt was a spectacular failure."

Eeks - An expression of surprise or fear.
"Eeks! That scared me!"
Translation: "Ah! That scared me!"

Endgame - Ultimate goal or conclusion.
"Winning the championship is the endgame."

Translation: "Winning the championship is the ultimate goal."

Ew - Disgust or distaste.
"Ew, that's gross!"
Translation: "That's disgusting!"

Ex - Former significant other.
"I ran into my ex at the store."
Translation: "I saw my former significant other at the store."

Eccentric - Unconventional or quirky.
"He's an eccentric artist."
Translation: "He's an unconventional artist."

Emo - Emotionally sensitive or dramatic.
"He's so emo about everything."
Translation: "He's so emotionally sensitive about everything."

Enthused - Excited or enthusiastic.
"She was really enthused about the project."
Translation: "She was really excited about the project."

Epicenter - Central point of something.
"The club is the epicenter of nightlife."
Translation: "The club is the central point of nightlife."

Euphoric - Extremely happy or joyful.
"I felt euphoric after the concert."
Translation: "I felt extremely happy after the concert."

Envy - Jealousy or desire.
"She looked at his new car with envy."
Translation: "She looked at his new car with jealousy."

Eerie - Strange and frightening.
"The abandoned house was eerie."
Translation: "The abandoned house was strange and frightening."

Exhausted - Very tired.
"I'm exhausted after that workout."
Translation: "I'm very tired after that workout."

Eureka - A cry of joy or satisfaction when one finds or discovers something.
"Eureka! I found my keys!"
Translation: "I found my keys!"

Epicure - A person who takes particular pleasure in fine food and drink.
"He's an epicure who loves gourmet food."
Translation: "He's a person who loves gourmet food."

F

FOMO - Fear of missing out.
"I have FOMO about missing the party."
Translation: "I have fear of missing out on the party."

Flex - To show off.
"He's always flexing his new car."
Translation: "He's always showing off his new car."

Fam - Family or close friends.
"What's up, fam?"
Translation: "What's up, family?"

Flake - To cancel plans last minute.
"She flaked on our dinner plans."
Translation: "She canceled our dinner plans last minute."

Fresh - Cool or stylish.
"Those shoes are fresh!"
Translation: "Those shoes are cool!"

Finesse - To handle something skillfully.
"He finessed his way out of trouble."
Translation: "He skillfully handled his way out of trouble."

Freak out - To become very anxious or afraid.
"Don't freak out, it's just a spider."
Translation: "Don't become very anxious, it's just a spider."

Fly - Stylish or attractive.
"She looks so fly in that outfit."

Translation: "She looks so stylish in that outfit."
Flex - To show off.
"He loves to flex his muscles."
Translation: "He loves to show off his muscles."

Full of it - Lying or exaggerating.
"He's so full of it, I don't believe him."
Translation: "He's lying, I don't believe him."

Funk - A state of depression.
"I've been in a funk lately."
Translation: "I've been in a state of depression lately."

Fizz - Energy or excitement.
"The party had a lot of fizz."
Translation: "The party had a lot of excitement."

Feisty - Lively and spirited.
"She's so feisty when she's challenged."
Translation: "She's so lively when she's challenged."

Flunk - To fail.
"I can't flunk this exam."
Translation: "I can't fail this exam."

Flip out - To lose control or become very excited.
"She flipped out when she won the lottery."
Translation: "She lost control when she won the lottery."

Freak - A person who is obsessed with something.
"He's a fitness freak."
Translation: "He's obsessed with fitness."

Funky - Strange or unusual.
"This smell is really funky."
Translation: "This smell is really strange."

Fuzz - Police officers.
"The fuzz showed up at the party."
Translation: "The police officers showed up at the party."

Famished - Extremely hungry.
"I’m famished, let’s eat."
Translation: "I’m extremely hungry, let’s eat."

Flat-out - Completely or absolutely.
"He flat-out denied the allegations."
Translation: "He completely denied the allegations."

G

G.O.A.T. - Greatest of all time.
"Michael Jordan is the G.O.A.T. of basketball."
Translation: "Michael Jordan is the greatest of all time in basketball."

Ghost - To suddenly cut off all communication.
"She ghosted me after our date."
Translation: "She suddenly cut off all communication after our date."

Gig - A job or booking.
"I have a gig at the club tonight."
Translation: "I have a job at the club tonight."

Grill - To question intensely.
"My parents grilled me about my grades."
Translation: "My parents questioned me intensely about my grades."

Grub - Food.
"Let's get some grub."
Translation: "Let's get some food."

Gutsy - Brave or daring.
"That was a gutsy move."
Translation: "That was a brave move."

Goofy - Silly or ridiculous.
"Stop being so goofy."
Translation: "Stop being so silly."

Glam - Glamorous.
"She looks so glam tonight."
Translation: "She looks so glamorous tonight."

Gamer - Someone who plays video games.
"He's a serious gamer."
Translation: "He's very into video games."

Gassed - Tired or exhausted.
"I'm gassed after that workout."
Translation: "I'm tired after that workout."

Giddy - Extremely happy.
"She was giddy with excitement."
Translation: "She was extremely happy with excitement."

Grit - Courage or resolve.
"He showed a lot of grit in the competition."
Translation: "He showed a lot of courage in the competition."

Glow up - A significant transformation.
"She had a major glow up over the summer."
Translation: "She had a significant transformation over the summer."

Grind - Hard work or effort.
"Keep up the grind, and you'll succeed."
Translation: "Keep up the hard work, and you'll succeed."

Grimy - Dirty or unpleasant.
"This place is so grimy."
Translation: "This place is so dirty."

Groovy - Cool or fashionable.
"That's a groovy outfit."
Translation: "That's a cool outfit."

Gag - A joke or trick.
"It was just a gag."
Translation: "It was just a joke."

Guzzle - To drink quickly.
"He guzzled down the soda."
Translation: "He drank the soda quickly."

Gritty - Showing courage and resolve.
"The movie was gritty and realistic."
Translation: "The movie showed courage and was realistic."

Grouchy - In a bad mood.
"He's always so grouchy in the morning."
Translation: "He's always in a bad mood in the morning."

H

Hype - Excitement or enthusiasm.
"The hype for the new game is real."
Translation: "The excitement for the new game is real."

Hangry - Hungry and angry.
"I get so hangry if I don't eat."
Translation: "I get so angry if I don't eat."

High-key - Openly or obviously.
"I high-key want to go to that concert."
Translation: "I openly want to go to that concert."

Hundo P - 100%, absolutely.
"I'm hundo P sure about this."
Translation: "I'm 100% sure about this."

Hot mess - A person or thing in disarray.
"She's a hot mess after that breakup."
Translation: "She's in disarray after that breakup."

Hitched - Married.
"They got hitched last weekend."
Translation: "They got married last weekend."

Hustle - To work hard or move quickly.
"You need to hustle to finish on time."
Translation: "You need to work hard to finish on time."

Hyped - Extremely excited.
"I'm so hyped for the party!"
Translation: "I'm extremely excited for the party!"

Hater - Someone who dislikes or criticizes.
"Ignore the haters, keep doing you."
Translation: "Ignore the people who dislike you, keep being yourself."

Hip - Cool or trendy.
"That new café is so hip."
Translation: "That new café is so trendy."

Holla - To call out or shout.
"Holla if you need help."
Translation: "Shout if you need help."

Hundo - Short for hundred.
"I'll pay you back a hundo."
Translation: "I'll pay you back a hundred."

Hyped up - Excited or enthusiastic.
"He was hyped up for the game."
Translation: "He was excited for the game."

Holla back - To respond.
"Holla back when you get a chance."
Translation: "Respond when you get a chance."

Hard pass - A definite rejection.
"That's a hard pass for me."
Translation: "That's a definite rejection for me."

Homie - A close friend.
"What's up, homie?"
Translation: "What's up, friend?"

Hit me up - Contact me.
"Hit me up later."
Translation: "Contact me later."

Head over heels - Deeply in love.
"She's head over heels for him."
Translation: "She's deeply in love with him."

Hang loose - Relax and take it easy.
"Just hang loose and enjoy your vacation."
Translation: "Just relax and enjoy your vacation."

Hustler - Someone who works hard to achieve goals.
"He's a real hustler, always grinding."
Translation: "He's someone who works hard to achieve goals, always grinding."

I

Iffy - Uncertain or questionable.
"I'm feeling iffy about this plan."
Translation: "I'm feeling uncertain about this plan."

Ice - Expensive jewelry.
"Check out his new ice."
Translation: "Check out his new expensive jewelry."

In the loop - Informed or updated.
"Keep me in the loop."
Translation: "Keep me informed."

I'm down - I agree or I'm interested.
"Want to go out tonight? I'm down."
Translation: "Want to go out tonight? I'm interested."

In the zone - Fully focused.
"He's in the zone right now."
Translation: "He's fully focused right now."

In the bag - Assured success.
"The victory is in the bag."
Translation: "The victory is assured."

Insane - Extremely good or impressive.
"That trick was insane!"
Translation: "That trick was extremely impressive!"

In a pickle - In a difficult situation.
"I'm in a pickle with this problem."
Translation: "I'm in a difficult situation with this problem."

It’s lit - It’s exciting or fun.
"The party last night? It’s lit!"
Translation: "The party last night was exciting!"

I’m game - I’m willing to participate.
"You want to join us? I’m game."
Translation: "You want to join us? I’m willing to participate."

In the clear - Free from trouble.
"We’re in the clear now."
Translation: "We’re free from trouble now."

Ice cold - Very cold or unfriendly.
"Her response was ice cold."
Translation: "Her response was very unfriendly."

Iron out - To resolve or smooth out.
"Let’s iron out the details."
Translation: "Let’s resolve the details."

In a flash - Very quickly.
"I’ll be there in a flash."
Translation: "I’ll be there very quickly."

In the limelight - Receiving attention.
"She loves being in the limelight."
Translation: "She loves receiving attention."

I’m shook - I’m surprised or shocked.
"That news left me shook."
Translation: "That news left me surprised."

In the groove - Performing well.
"He’s in the groove today."
Translation: "He’s performing well today."

I’m out - I’m leaving.
"This is boring, I’m out."
Translation: "This is boring, I’m leaving."

In a jiffy - Very quickly.
"I’ll finish this in a jiffy."
Translation: "I’ll finish this very quickly."

It’s a wrap - It’s finished.
"Alright, it’s a wrap."
Translation: "Alright, it’s finished."

J

Jacked - Very muscular.
"He's jacked from all that weightlifting."
Translation: "He's very muscular from all that weightlifting."

Janky - Of poor quality.
"This phone is so janky."
Translation: "This phone is of poor quality."

Jive - Deceptive or insincere talk.
"Don't give me that jive."
Translation: "Don't give me that deceptive talk."

Juiced - Excited or pumped up.
"I'm juiced for the game tonight!"
Translation: "I'm excited for the game tonight!"

Jelly - Jealous.
"She's jelly of his new car."
Translation: "She's jealous of his new car."

Jam - A favorite song.
"This is my jam!"
Translation: "This is my favorite song!"

Jot - To write quickly.
"I'll jot down the notes."
Translation: "I'll write down the notes quickly."

Jack up - To increase or raise.
"They jacked up the prices."

Translation: "They raised the prices."
Juggle - To manage multiple tasks.
"I'm juggling too many projects."
Translation: "I'm managing too many projects."

Jazzed - Excited or enthusiastic.
"I'm jazzed about the concert."
Translation: "I'm excited about the concert."

Junkie - An addict.
"He's a TV junkie."
Translation: "He's addicted to watching TV."

Jolt - A sudden surprise or shock.
"The news gave me a jolt."
Translation: "The news gave me a surprise."

Jam-packed - Very full or crowded.
"The train was jam-packed."
Translation: "The train was very full."

Jacked up - Broken or messed up.
"My car is jacked up."
Translation: "My car is broken."

Jit - A young person or teenager.
"He's just a jit."
Translation: "He's just a teenager."

Jive turkey - A person who is unreliable or a liar.
"Don't be a jive turkey."
Translation: "Don't be unreliable."

Juiced up - Filled with energy or enthusiasm.
"He's all juiced up for the race."
Translation: "He's filled with energy for the race."

Jaw-dropping - Astonishing or amazing.
"The view was jaw-dropping."
Translation: "The view was amazing."

Jiffy - A very short amount of time.
"I'll be back in a jiffy."
Translation: "I'll be back very soon."

Jive - To speak or act in a nonsensical manner.
"Stop talking jive."
Translation: "Stop talking nonsense."

K

Kudos - Praise or credit.
"Kudos for a job well done."
Translation: "Praise for a job well done."

Kick back - To relax.
"Let's kick back and watch a movie."
Translation: "Let's relax and watch a movie."

Killer - Excellent or impressive.
"That was a killer performance."
Translation: "That was an excellent performance."

Keep it real - Be honest or genuine.
"Just keep it real with me."
Translation: "Just be honest with me."

Knockout - A very attractive person.
"She's an absolute knockout."
Translation: "She's very attractive."

Kicks - Shoes."Nice kicks!"
Translation: "Nice shoes!"
Knock it off - Stop doing that.

"**Knock it off,** you're being annoying."
Translation: "Stop doing that, you're being annoying."

Kooky - Strange or eccentric.
"He's a bit kooky."
Translation: "He's a bit strange."

Knit-pick - To find small faults.
"Stop knit-picking and enjoy the show."
Translation: "Stop finding small faults and enjoy the show."

Kinky - Unusual or unconventional.
"They have some kinky interests."
Translation: "They have some unusual interests."

Kooky - Quirky or eccentric.
"She has a kooky sense of humor."
Translation: "She has a quirky sense of humor."

Knock it out of the park - To do something exceptionally well.
"You really knocked it out of the park with that presentation."
Translation: "You did exceptionally well with that presentation."

Kaleidoscope - A complex mix of colors or patterns.
"The city lights were a kaleidoscope of colors."
Translation: "The city lights were a complex mix of colors."

Keep your cool - Stay calm.
"Even in stressful situations, he keeps his cool."
Translation: "Even in stressful situations, he stays calm."

Knee-jerk reaction - A quick and automatic response.
"His comment was a knee-jerk reaction."
Translation: "His comment was a quick response."

Kiss and tell - To reveal private information.

"I don't kiss and tell."
Translation: "I don't reveal private information."

Keen - Enthusiastic or eager.
"She's keen to learn new things."
Translation: "She's enthusiastic to learn new things."

Keep it on the down-low - Keep it secret.
"Let's keep this on the down-low."
Translation: "Let's keep this secret."

Karma - The concept of cause and effect.
"He believes in good karma."
Translation: "He believes in the concept of cause and effect."

Knuckle down - To focus and work hard.
"It's time to knuckle down and study."
Translation: "It's time to focus and study."

L

Lit - Exciting or excellent.
"The party was lit!"
Translation: "The party was exciting!"

Low-key - Slightly or secretly.
"I'm low-key interested in that class."
Translation: "I'm slightly interested in that class."

LOL - Laugh out loud.
"That joke made me LOL."
Translation: "That joke made me laugh out loud."

Lame - Unimpressive or boring.
"That movie was lame."
Translation: "That movie was unimpressive."

Legit - Legitimate or real.
"This offer seems legit."
Translation: "This offer seems real."

Lag - To be slow or delayed.
"My computer is lagging."
Translation: "My computer is slow."

Lingo - Language or terminology.
"Do you understand the lingo?"
Translation: "Do you understand the language?"

Lush - Luxurious or rich.
"This place is so lush."
Translation: "This place is so luxurious."

Lit AF - Extremely exciting.
"The concert was lit AF."
Translation: "The concert was extremely exciting."

LIT - Lost in translation.
"Some jokes are LIT."
Translation: "Some jokes are lost in translation."

Legit - Authentic or real.
"That's a legit offer."
Translation: "That's an authentic offer."

Loner - Someone who prefers to be alone.
"He's a bit of a loner."
Translation: "He prefers to be alone."

Lame-o - Someone who is boring or dull.
"Don't be a lame-o."
Translation: "Don't be boring."

Lush - Luxurious or appealing.
"The garden is so lush."
Translation: "The garden is so appealing."

Lean - To incline or favor something.
"I'm leaning towards that option."
Translation: "I'm favoring that option."

Lowdown - The true facts or information.
"Give me the lowdown on what happened."
Translation: "Give me the true facts on what happened."

Livid - Extremely angry.
"He was livid about the news."
Translation: "He was extremely angry about the news."

Lively - Full of energy.
"The party was lively."
Translation: "The party was full of energy."

Laid-back - Relaxed or easygoing.
"He's very laid-back."
Translation: "He's very relaxed."

Loaded - Rich or wealthy.
"He's loaded with cash."
Translation: "He's rich."

M

MVP - Most valuable player.
"She's the MVP of the team."
Translation: "She's the most valuable player of the team."

Mood - Relatable feeling or situation.
"That's such a mood."
Translation: "That's such a relatable feeling."

Mad - Very or extremely.
"That's mad cool."
Translation: "That's extremely cool."

MIA - Missing in action.
"He's been MIA for days."
Translation: "He's been missing for days."

Meh - Indifference or lack of interest.
"That movie was meh."
Translation: "That movie was uninteresting."

Mint - Perfect or excellent.
"This car is in mint condition."
Translation: "This car is in excellent condition."

Munchies - A craving for snacks.
"I've got the munchies."
Translation: "I'm craving snacks."

Mojo - Personal charm or magnetism.
"I lost my mojo."
Translation: "I lost my charm."

Make bank - To earn a lot of money.
"He's making bank with his new job."
Translation: "He's earning a lot of money with his new job."

Mug - Face.
"Wipe that grin off your mug."
Translation: "Wipe that grin off your face."

Mic drop - A definitive or impressive statement.
"And that's how it's done. Mic drop."
Translation: "And that's how it's done. Impressive."

Mind-blowing - Astonishing or amazing.
"That performance was mind-blowing."
Translation: "That performance was amazing."

Messy - Chaotic or disorganized.
"Her room is so messy."
Translation: "Her room is so disorganized."

Maxed out - Fully used or exhausted.
"I'm maxed out on credit."
Translation: "I'm fully used on credit."

Man cave - A room or space for a man.
"He's in his man cave."
Translation: "He's in his personal space."

Moody - Easily upset or annoyed.
"She's been moody lately."
Translation: "She's been easily upset lately."

Motormouth - Someone who talks a lot.
"He's a real motormouth."
Translation: "He talks a lot."

Mess around - To waste time or act playfully.
"Stop messing around and get to work."
Translation: "Stop wasting time and get to work."

Mooch - To take advantage of someone.
"He's always mooching off his friends."
Translation: "He's always taking advantage of his friends."

Mashup - A mix of different elements.
"The DJ played a great mashup."
Translation: "The DJ played a great mix."

N

Noob - Beginner or novice.
"He's a noob at this game."
Translation: "He's a beginner at this game."

Nailed it - Completed perfectly.
"You nailed it!"
Translation: "You completed it perfectly!"

Nosh - To snack or eat.
"Let's nosh on something."
Translation: "Let's snack on something."

Netflix and chill - Watch Netflix with romantic intentions.
"Want to Netflix and chill?"
Translation: "Want to watch Netflix with romantic intentions?"

Nifty - Clever or useful.
"That's a nifty gadget."
Translation: "That's a clever gadget."

Nuke - To destroy or obliterate.
"They nuked the old building."
Translation: "They destroyed the old building."

Nerd - A person who is very interested in a subject.
"He's a science nerd."
Translation: "He's very interested in science."

No sweat - No problem or easy.
"It's no sweat, I can handle it."

Translation: "It's no problem, I can handle it."

Nod off - To fall asleep.
"I nodded off during the movie."
Translation: "I fell asleep during the movie."

Nippy - Cold or chilly.
"It's a bit nippy outside."
Translation: "It's a bit cold outside."

Nuke - To heat in a microwave.
"Just nuke it for a minute."
Translation: "Just heat it in the microwave for a minute."

Naysayer - A person who opposes or criticizes.
"Don't listen to the naysayers."
Translation: "Don't listen to the critics."

Nifty - Attractive or stylish.
"That's a nifty jacket."
Translation: "That's a stylish jacket."

Nugget - A small piece of valuable information.
"He gave me a nugget of advice."
Translation: "He gave me a valuable piece of advice."

Newbie - A newcomer or beginner.
"She's a newbie in the team."
Translation: "She's a newcomer in the team."

Night owl - A person who stays up late.
"I'm a night owl, I work best at night."
Translation: "I stay up late, I work best at night."

Nifty - Ingenious or clever.
"That's a nifty solution."
Translation: "That's a clever solution."

Nuke - To eliminate completely.
"They nuked the problem in no time."
Translation: "They eliminated the problem quickly."

Nutty - Crazy or foolish.
"That idea is nutty."
Translation: "That idea is crazy."

Nail - To achieve perfectly.
"You nailed the presentation."
Translation: "You achieved the presentation perfectly."

O

OMG - Oh my God.
"OMG, I can't believe it!"
Translation: "Oh my God, I can't believe it!"

On fleek - Perfectly done.
"Her makeup is on fleek."
Translation: "Her makeup is perfectly done."

Over the moon - Extremely happy.
"She's over the moon about her new job."
Translation: "She's extremely happy about her new job."

Off the hook - Free from responsibility or outstanding.
"That party was off the hook!"
Translation: "That party was outstanding!"

Out of the blue - Unexpectedly.
"He called me out of the blue."
Translation: "He called me unexpectedly."

On point - Exactly right.
"Your presentation was on point."
Translation: "Your presentation was exactly right."

On the ball - Alert and competent.
"She's really on the ball."
Translation: "She's very alert and competent."

Offbeat - Unconventional.
"He has an offbeat sense of humor."
Translation: "He has an unconventional sense of humor."

Off the charts - Beyond normal limits.
"Her energy level is off the charts."
Translation: "Her energy level is beyond normal limits."

On the go - Busy or active.
"I'm always on the go."
Translation: "I'm always busy."

Out of this world - Extraordinary.
"The food was out of this world."
Translation: "The food was extraordinary."

On cloud nine - Very happy.
"He's on cloud nine after winning the game."
Translation: "He's very happy after winning the game."

On the same page - In agreement.
"We're finally on the same page."
Translation: "We're finally in agreement."

Out of the loop - Not informed.
"I feel out of the loop."
Translation: "I feel not informed."

On a roll - Having a series of successes.
"She's on a roll lately."
Translation: "She's having a series of successes lately."

Off the wall - Bizarre or unconventional.
"His ideas are off the wall."
Translation: "His ideas are unconventional."

On the up and up - Honest and legal.

"Everything is on the up and up."
Translation: "Everything is honest and legal."

Over the top - Excessive.
"That's a bit over the top."
Translation: "That's a bit excessive."

On the fly - Quickly and spontaneously.
"We made the decision on the fly."
Translation: "We made the decision quickly."

Off the grid - Untraceable or not connected.
"They're living off the grid."
Translation: "They're living untraceable."

P

Party pooper - A person who spoils the fun.
"Don't be a party pooper."
Translation: "Don't spoil the fun."

Pumpkin - A term of endearment.
"How's my little pumpkin?"
Translation: "How's my dear?"

Phat - Excellent or cool.
"That's a phat beat!"
Translation: "That's an excellent beat!"

Psyched - Excited and enthusiastic.
"I'm psyched for the concert!"
Translation: "I'm excited for the concert!"

Piece of cake - Very easy.
"This task is a piece of cake."
Translation: "This task is very easy."

Pop - To visit briefly.
"I'll pop by your place later."
Translation: "I'll visit your place briefly later."

Props - Respect or recognition.
"Give her props for her hard work."
Translation: "Give her respect for her hard work."

Peachy - Very good or fine.
"Everything is just peachy."
Translation: "Everything is very good."

Punk - A young troublemaker.
"He's just a punk."
Translation: "He's just a young troublemaker."

Posh - Elegant or luxurious.
"That's a posh hotel."
Translation: "That's an elegant hotel."

Play it by ear - To improvise.
"Let's play it by ear."
Translation: "Let's improvise."

Power nap - A short sleep.
"I need a power nap."
Translation: "I need a short sleep."

Put a lid on it - To stop talking.
"Put a lid on it, please."
Translation: "Stop talking, please."

Pumped - Full of energy.
"I'm pumped for the game."
Translation: "I'm full of energy for the game."

Pig out - To eat a lot.
"We pigged out at the buffet."
Translation: "We ate a lot at the buffet."

Pumped up - Excited.
"I'm pumped up for the event."
Translation: "I'm excited for the event."

Pass the buck - To avoid responsibility.
"Don't pass the buck."
Translation: "Don't avoid responsibility."

Put on blast - To publicly criticize.
"She put him on blast on social media."
Translation: "She publicly criticized him on social media."

Pat on the back - Praise or recognition.
"Give yourself a pat on the back."
Translation: "Give yourself praise."

Pick-me-up - Something that improves mood.
"I need a coffee for a pick-me-up."
Translation: "I need a coffee to improve my mood."

Q

Quirky - Unconventional or eccentric.
"He has a quirky sense of style."
Translation: "He has an unconventional sense of style."

Quip - A witty remark.
"She always has a quip ready."
Translation: "She always has a witty remark ready."

Queen bee - The leader of a group.
"She’s the queen bee of the school."
Translation: "She’s the leader of the school."

Quaint - Charming in an old-fashioned way.
"They live in a quaint cottage."
Translation: "They live in a charming cottage."

Quickie - Something done quickly.
"Let’s have a quickie meeting."
Translation: "Let’s have a quick meeting."

Quibble - To argue over minor issues.
"They quibble over everything."
Translation: "They argue over minor issues."

Quirky - Odd or unusual.
"Her behavior is quite quirky."
Translation: "Her behavior is quite odd."

Q-tip - To clean with a cotton swab.
"I need to Q-tip my ears."
Translation: "I need to clean my ears with a cotton swab."

Quicksand - A tricky situation.
"We're in quicksand now."
Translation: "We're in a tricky situation now."

Quarterback - To lead or organize.
"He quarterbacked the project."
Translation: "He led the project."

Quizzical - Puzzled or questioning.
"She gave me a quizzical look."
Translation: "She gave me a puzzled look."

Quipster - Someone who makes jokes.
"He's such a quipster."
Translation: "He's always making jokes."

Quench - To satisfy a thirst.
"I need to quench my thirst."
Translation: "I need to satisfy my thirst."

Queue up - To line up.
"Let's queue up for tickets."
Translation: "Let's line up for tickets."

Quench - To extinguish or end.
"Quench the fire quickly."
Translation: "Extinguish the fire quickly."

Quitter - Someone who gives up easily.
"Don't be a quitter."
Translation: "Don't give up easily."

Quash - To suppress or put an end to.
"The rebellion was quashed."
Translation: "The rebellion was suppressed."

Quirky - Characterized by peculiar traits.
"She has a quirky charm."
Translation: "She has a peculiar charm."

Quibble - To raise minor objections.
"They quibble over the details."
Translation: "They raise minor objections over the details."

Queue - A line or sequence.
"There's a long queue for the concert."
Translation: "There's a long line for the concert."

R

Rad - Cool or awesome.
"That's a rad skateboard."
Translation: "That's a cool skateboard."

Rock on - Continue with enthusiasm.
"Rock on with your project!"
Translation: "Continue with enthusiasm with your project!"

Rip-off - Something overpriced.
"This shirt is a rip-off."
Translation: "This shirt is overpriced."

Rave - To give enthusiastic praise.
"She raved about the new restaurant."
Translation: "She gave enthusiastic praise about the new restaurant."

Razz - To tease or mock.
"They razzed him for his new haircut."
Translation: "They teased him for his new haircut."

Roll out - To launch or introduce.
"They're rolling out a new product."
Translation: "They're launching a new product."

Ripped - Having well-defined muscles.
"He's really ripped."
Translation: "He has well-defined muscles."

R&R - Rest and relaxation.

"I need some R&R this weekend."
Translation: "I need some rest and relaxation this weekend."

Roast - To criticize humorously.
"They roasted him at the party."
Translation: "They criticized him humorously at the party."

Rugrat - A young child.
"The rugrats are playing outside."
Translation: "The young children are playing outside."

Rekt - Destroyed or ruined.
"He got rekt in the game."
Translation: "He got ruined in the game."

Radical - Extreme or revolutionary.
"That's a radical idea."
Translation: "That's an extreme idea."

Rave - A dance party.
"We're going to a rave tonight."
Translation: "We're going to a dance party tonight."

Rip - To move quickly.
"He ripped through the crowd."
Translation: "He moved quickly through the crowd."

Retro - Style from the past.
"She loves retro fashion."
Translation: "She loves fashion from the past."

Rave - To speak wildly.

"He raved about the incident."
Translation: "He spoke wildly about the incident."

Rough - Difficult or harsh.
"It's been a rough day."
Translation: "It's been a difficult day."

Rad - Excellent or impressive.
"That's a rad performance."
Translation: "That's an impressive performance."

Run-of-the-mill - Ordinary or average.
"The movie was run-of-the-mill."
Translation: "The movie was ordinary."

Racket – A loud noise or commotion.
"What's all the racket?"
Translation: "What's all the noise?"

S

Savage - Fierce or brutal.
"That was a savage comeback."
Translation: "That was a fierce comeback."

Slay - To impress greatly.
"You slayed that performance!"
Translation: "You impressed greatly with that performance!"

Sick - Awesome or cool.
"That trick was sick!"
Translation: "That trick was awesome!"

Salty - Bitter or upset.
"He's salty about losing the game."
Translation: "He's bitter about losing the game."

Ship - To support a romantic pairing.
"I ship those two characters."
Translation: "I support the romantic pairing of those two characters."

Snafu - A chaotic or confused situation.
"The event was a snafu."
Translation: "The event was chaotic."

Swag - Cool style or appearance.
"He's got swag."
Translation: "He's got cool style."

Spill the tea - To gossip or share secrets.
"Let's spill the tea about what happened."
Translation: "Let's gossip about what happened."

Stan - An overzealous fan.
"I stan that band."
Translation: "I'm an overzealous fan of that band."

Shook - Surprised or shocked.
"I'm still shook by the news."
Translation: "I'm still shocked by the news."

Squad - A close group of friends.
"I'm hanging out with my squad."
Translation: "I'm hanging out with my close group of friends."

Shade - Disrespect or criticism.
"She threw shade at him."
Translation: "She disrespected him."

Savvy - Knowledgeable or well-informed.
"She's very tech-savvy."
Translation: "She's very knowledgeable about technology."

Snazzy - Stylish or attractive.
"That's a snazzy outfit."
Translation: "That's a stylish outfit."

Stoked - Excited or enthusiastic.
"I'm stoked for the trip."
Translation: "I'm excited for the trip."

Swole - Muscular or buff.
"He’s looking swole."
Translation: "He’s looking muscular."

Squabble - A minor argument.
"They had a squabble over the details."
Translation: "They had a minor argument over the details."

Simp - Someone who does too much for someone they like.
"He’s such a simp for her."
Translation: "He does too much for her."

Slap - To be excellent.
"This song slaps!"
Translation: "This song is excellent!"

Suss - To figure out.
"I need to suss out the situation."
Translation: "I need to figure out the situation."

T

Throw shade - To subtly insult.
"She's always throwing shade."
Translation: "She's always subtly insulting."

Tea - Gossip or personal information.
"What's the tea?"
Translation: "What's the gossip?"

Turnt - Excited or hyped.
"This party is turnt!"
Translation: "This party is exciting!"

Thirsty - Desperate for attention.
"He's so thirsty for likes."
Translation: "He's so desperate for attention."

Trash - To criticize harshly.
"She trashed his performance."
Translation: "She criticized his performance harshly."

Totes - Totally.
"I'm totes excited."
Translation: "I'm totally excited."

Throwback - Something nostalgic.
"This song is a throwback."
Translation: "This song is nostalgic."

Trendy - Fashionable or in style.
"That's a trendy outfit."
Translation: "That's a fashionable outfit."

Troll - To deliberately provoke.
"He's trolling on the forums."
Translation: "He's deliberately provoking on the forums."

Tight - Close or intimate.
"We're really tight."
Translation: "We're really close."

Trippin' - Acting crazy.
"Why are you trippin'?"
Translation: "Why are you acting crazy?"

Trill - True and real.
"She's so trill."
Translation: "She's so genuine."

Twerk - A type of dance.
"She loves to twerk."
Translation: "She loves that type of dance."

TMI - Too much information.
"That's TMI."
Translation: "That's too much information."

Twinning - Matching or alike.
"We're twinning today!"
Translation: "We're matching today!"

Thug - A violent person.
"He's a thug."
Translation: "He's a violent person."

Tattle - To report someone's wrongdoing.
"Don't tattle on your friends."
Translation: "Don't report your friends' wrongdoing."

Talk smack - To speak insultingly.
"He's always talking smack."
Translation: "He's always speaking insultingly."

Tap out - To give up.
"I'm about to tap out."
Translation: "I'm about to give up."

Tight - Excellent or cool.
"That's a tight beat."
Translation: "That's an excellent beat."

U

Unreal - Amazing or unbelievable.
"That concert was unreal."
Translation: "That concert was amazing."

Uber - Extremely.
"She's uber talented."
Translation: "She's extremely talented."

Unplug - To disconnect or take a break.
"I need to unplug this weekend."
Translation: "I need to take a break this weekend."

Uptight - Anxious or tense.
"He's always so uptight."
Translation: "He's always so anxious."

Under the weather - Feeling ill.
"I'm feeling under the weather today."
Translation: "I'm feeling ill today."

Up in the air - Uncertain.
"Our plans are up in the air."
Translation: "Our plans are uncertain."

Upgrade - To improve.
"Time to upgrade your phone."
Translation: "Time to improve your phone."

Uncool - Not fashionable or acceptable.
"That's so uncool."
Translation: "That's not fashionable."

Unfriend - To remove from a friend list.
"I had to unfriend him."
Translation: "I had to remove him from my friend list."

Uber - To use the Uber service.
"Let's Uber to the party."
Translation: "Let's use the Uber service to go to the party."

Under wraps - Secret or hidden.
"Keep it under wraps."
Translation: "Keep it secret."

Unplugged - Acoustic or without amplification.
"I love their unplugged performance."
Translation: "I love their acoustic performance."

Unwind - To relax.
"I need to unwind after work."
Translation: "I need to relax after work."

Upbeat - Cheerful or optimistic.
"She's always upbeat."
Translation: "She's always cheerful."

Upgrade - A better version.
"This is a major upgrade."
Translation: "This is a better version."

U-turn - A complete change of direction.
"He made a U-turn on his decision."
Translation: "He completely changed his decision."

Unhinged - Mentally unstable.
"He's acting unhinged."
Translation: "He's acting mentally unstable."

Upcycle - To reuse creatively.
"I upcycled an old dresser."
Translation: "I creatively reused an old dresser."

Unfiltered - Honest or direct.
"She gave an unfiltered opinion."
Translation: "She gave an honest opinion."

Up to speed - Fully informed.
"Bring me up to speed."
Translation: "Fully inform me."

V

Vibe - Atmosphere or feeling.
"This place has a good vibe."
Translation: "This place has a good atmosphere."

Viral - Quickly popularized online.
"That video went viral."
Translation: "That video became quickly popular."

Vanilla - Plain or ordinary.
"The design is too vanilla."
Translation: "The design is too plain."

Vibes - Emotional states or energies.
"I'm getting good vibes from this."
Translation: "I'm getting good energies from this."

Vlog - A video blog.
"She started a vlog about travel."
Translation: "She started a video blog about travel."

Vamoose - To leave quickly.
"Let's vamoose from here."
Translation: "Let's leave quickly from here."

Veg out - To relax lazily.
"I'm going to veg out this weekend."
Translation: "I'm going to relax lazily this weekend."

Vexed - Annoyed or frustrated.
"I'm vexed by the delay."
Translation: "I'm annoyed by the delay."

Vibes - Sensations or feelings.
"She has great vibes."
Translation: "She has great feelings."

Viable - Feasible or practical.
"Is this plan viable?"
Translation: "Is this plan feasible?"

Vanity - Excessive pride.
"His vanity is annoying."
Translation: "His excessive pride is annoying."

Vent - To express frustration.
"I need to vent about my day."
Translation: "I need to express my frustration about my day."

Vivid - Bright or clear.
"I have a vivid memory of it."
Translation: "I have a clear memory of it."

Vintage - Classic or old-fashioned.
"I love vintage clothing."
Translation: "I love old-fashioned clothing."

Virgo - Astrological sign.
"She's a Virgo."
Translation: "She's born under the Virgo sign."

Vista - A scenic view.
"This hotel has a great vista."
Translation: "This hotel has a great view."

Vogue - Fashionable.
"That style is in vogue."
Translation: "That style is fashionable."

Vivid - Detailed or realistic.
"She gave a vivid description."
Translation: "She gave a detailed description."

Virtual - Simulated or online.
"We had a virtual meeting."
Translation: "We had an online meeting."

Volatile - Unstable or unpredictable.
"The market is volatile."
Translation: "The market is unstable."

W

Wack - Strange or weird.
"That movie was wack."
Translation: "That movie was strange."

Wasted - Intoxicated.
"He got wasted at the party."
Translation: "He got intoxicated at the party."

Wavy - Cool or awesome.
"That song is wavy."
Translation: "That song is cool."

Whack - Bad or poor quality.
"This food is whack."
Translation: "This food is poor quality."

Woke - Socially aware.
"She's really woke."
Translation: "She's really socially aware."

Whip - A car.
"Check out my new whip."
Translation: "Check out my new car."

Woah - Expression of surprise.
"Woah, that's amazing!"
Translation: "That's amazing!"

Wired - Full of energy.
"I'm wired from the coffee."

Translation: "I'm full of energy from the coffee."

Wing it - To improvise.
"I'll just wing it."
Translation: "I'll just improvise."

Whip up - To quickly prepare.
"I'll whip up some dinner."
Translation: "I'll quickly prepare some dinner."

Wonky - Unstable or shaky.
"This table is wonky."
Translation: "This table is unstable."

Word - Agreement or truth.
"Word, that's right."
Translation: "That's right."

Waffle - To be indecisive.
"Stop waffling and decide."
Translation: "Stop being indecisive and decide."

Whizz - To move quickly.
"He whizzed by me."
Translation: "He moved quickly by me."

Whiny - Complaining a lot.
"Stop being so whiny."
Translation: "Stop complaining a lot."

Whiz - Expert or genius.
"He's a math whiz."

Translation: "He's a math expert."

Wacky - Crazy or eccentric.
"That idea is wacky."
Translation: "That idea is crazy."

Wham - Sudden impact.
"Wham, it hit me!"
Translation: "It hit me suddenly!"

Woke - Aware of injustice.
"Stay woke."
Translation: "Stay aware of injustice."

Woot - Expression of excitement.
"Woot, we won!"
Translation: "We won!"

X

X-ray - To examine closely.
"Let's X-ray this plan."
Translation: "Let's examine this plan closely."

X-factor - Special quality.
"She has the X-factor."
Translation: "She has a special quality."

Xenial - Hospitable or friendly.
"They were very xenial."
Translation: "They were very hospitable."

Xerox - To copy.
"Can you Xerox these papers?"
Translation: "Can you copy these papers?"

X-rated - Explicit content.
"That movie is X-rated."
Translation: "That movie has explicit content."

X-out - To delete or cancel.
"X-out that mistake."
Translation: "Delete that mistake."

Xenophobia - Fear of foreigners.
"Xenophobia is a serious issue."
Translation: "Fear of foreigners is a serious issue."

Xylophone - Musical instrument.
"She plays the xylophone."
Translation: "She plays that musical instrument."

X-citing - Exciting.
"This news is X-citing!"
Translation: "This news is exciting!"

X-pert - Expert.
"He's an X-pert in his field."
Translation: "He's an expert in his field."

X-tra - Extra or more.
"I need X-tra time."
Translation: "I need more time."

X-treme - Extreme.
"That was an X-treme sport."
Translation: "That was an extreme sport."

X-press - Express.
"I need an X-press delivery."
Translation: "I need an express delivery."

X-hale - Exhale.
"X-hale and relax."
Translation: "Exhale and relax."

X-aggerate - Exaggerate.
"Don't X-aggerate."
Translation: "Don't exaggerate."

X-cel - Excel.
"She always X-cels in math."
Translation: "She always excels in math."

X-clusive - Exclusive.
"This is an X-clusive event."
Translation: "This is an exclusive event."

X-tend - Extend.
"X-tend your stay."
Translation: "Extend your stay."

X-hibit - Exhibit.
"That's a great X-hibit."
Translation: "That's a great exhibit."

X-act - Exact.
"I need the X-act amount."
Translation: "I need the exact amount."

Y

Yolo - You only live once.
"Let's go skydiving, YOLO!"
Translation: "Let's go skydiving, you only live once!"

Yas - Expression of excitement.
"Yas, I love it!"
Translation: "I love it!"

Yikes - Expression of concern.
"Yikes, that's scary."
Translation: "That's scary."

Yasss - Enthusiastic yes.
"Yasss, I'm so in!"
Translation: "I'm so in!"

Yawn - Boring.
"That movie was a yawn."
Translation: "That movie was boring."

Yeet - To throw.
"He yeeted the ball."
Translation: "He threw the ball."

Yap - To talk continuously.
"She won't stop yapping."
Translation: "She won't stop talking."

Yolo - To take a risk.
"I'm going for it, YOLO!"
Translation: "I'm taking a risk, you only live once!"

Yummy - Delicious.
"This cake is yummy."
Translation: "This cake is delicious."

Yak - To chat.
"We yakked for hours."
Translation: "We chatted for hours."

Yo - Hello or attention.
"Yo, over here!"
Translation: "Hello, over here!"

Yuck - Disgusting.
"This food is yuck."
Translation: "This food is disgusting."

Yummy - Attractive.
"He's so yummy."
Translation: "He's so attractive."

Yarn - A long story.
"She told a long yarn."
Translation: "She told a long story."

Yes-man - Someone who agrees to everything.
"Don't be a yes-man."
Translation: "Don't agree to everything."

Yahoo - Excitement.
"Yahoo, we did it!"
Translation: "We did it!"

Yearn - To desire.

"I yearn for adventure."
Translation: "I desire adventure."

Yield - To give in.
"He yielded to the pressure."
Translation: "He gave in to the pressure."

Yelp - A sharp cry.
"She let out a yelp."
Translation: "She let out a sharp cry."

Yolo - Live in the moment.
"Just do it, YOLO!"
Translation: "Live in the moment, you only live once!"

Z

Zoom - To move quickly.
"He zoomed past us."
Translation: "He moved quickly past us."

Zap - To eliminate.
"Zap that bug."
Translation: "Eliminate that bug."

Zonked - Extremely tired.
"I'm zonked after the trip."
Translation: "I'm extremely tired after the trip."

Zany - Wacky or eccentric.
"That comedian is zany."
Translation: "That comedian is eccentric."

Zing - A sharp remark.
"She gave a zing."
Translation: "She gave a sharp remark."

Zapped - Drained of energy.
"I'm zapped after the workout."
Translation: "I'm drained of energy after the workout."

Zeal - Enthusiasm.
"He has zeal for his work."
Translation: "He has enthusiasm for his work."

Zest - Liveliness or energy.
"She has zest for life."
Translation: "She has liveliness for life."

Zilch - Nothing or zero.
"I have zilch money."
Translation: "I have no money."

Zip - Energy or speed.
"He has zip in his step."
Translation: "He has energy in his step."

Zigzag - To move erratically.
"He zigzagged through the crowd."
Translation: "He moved erratically through the crowd."

Zoned out - Daydreaming or distracted.
"I zoned out during the lecture."
Translation: "I daydreamed during the lecture."

Zillion - An indefinitely large number.
"I have a zillion things to do."
Translation: "I have an indefinitely large number of things to do."

Zip it - Be quiet.
"Zip it, please!"
Translation: "Be quiet, please!"

Zesty - Spirited or energetic.
"He's a zesty person."
Translation: "He's a spirited person."

Zilch - Meaningless or unimportant.
"That's worth zilch."
Translation: "That's worth nothing."

Zone - Focus or concentration.
"Get in the zone."
Translation: "Focus."

Zany - Quirky or odd.
"His humor is zany."
Translation: "His humor is quirky."

Zippy - Fast or quick.
"He’s a zippy runner."
Translation: "He’s a fast runner."

Zen - Peaceful or calm.
"I’m feeling zen today."
Translation: "I’m feeling peaceful today."

Printed in Dunstable, United Kingdom

74270274R10047